MW00659428

By

Rev. Lawrence G. Lovasik, S.V.D.

C.B. P.C.

CATHOLIC BOOK PUBLISHING CORP.
New Jersey

NIHIL OBSTAT: Francis J. McAree, S.T.D.
Censor Librorum
IMPRIMATUR: ✠ Patrick J. Sheridan, D.D.
Vicar General, Archdiocese of New York

The Nihil Obstat and Imprimatur are official declarations that a book or pamphlet is free of doctrinal or moral error. No implication is contained therein that those who have granted the Nihil Obstat and Imprimatur agree with the contents, opinions or statements expressed.

CONTENTS

(T-30)

Printed in China
ISBN 978-0-89942-030-1
www.catholicbookpublishing.com

PREFACE

THERE are innumerable ways in which to pray and many methods of prayer. One of the greatest helps to prayer for most people is a book of prayers. It puts at our fingertips a precious treasury of words by which we can approach God every day. Such ready-made prayers imprint on our minds the sentiments that the Church wants us to have in prayer.

Prayers of this type also convey a deeper knowledge and understanding of the Church's teaching. In a subtle and unobtrusive fashion they teach the Faith while allowing us to approach God. By using them we not only come closer to God but also get to know Him better with every passing day.

It goes without saying that we can also pray in our words instead of words found on a printed page—and indeed we must do so. However, ready-made prayers are there for those times when we do not know what to say and need help in speaking to God. We need the help of past ages as well as present trends to say what we feel and what we should feel.

This book will help in disposing us to receive the Sacraments and to be united with God in the circumstances of life and celebrations of the mysteries of salvation during the Liturgical Year.

It also provides private devotions in honor of the Blessed Mother and the Saints, which are intended to lead us to God, the Source of holiness and Giver of every good gift.

THE MASS—OUR GREATEST PRAYER

Essence of the Mass

AT the Last Supper, our Savior instituted the Eucharistic sacrifice of His Body and Blood. He did this in order to perpetuate the sacrifice of the Cross throughout the centuries until He should come again.

Thus the Mass is:

(1) the *true sacrifice* of the New Covenant, in which a holy and living Victim is offered, Jesus Christ, and we in union with Him, as a gift of love and obedience to the Father;

(2) a *sacred meal* and *spiritual banquet* of the children of God;

(3) a *Paschal meal*, which evokes the passage (passover) of Jesus from this world to the Father; it renders Him present

and makes Him live again in souls, and anticipates our passage to the Kingdom of God;

(4) a *communitarian meal,* that is, a gathering together of the Head and His members, of Jesus and His Church, His Mystical Body, in order to carry out a perfect Divine worship.

Thus, the Mass is the greatest prayer we have. Through it we give thanks and praise to the Father for the wonderful future He has given us in His Son. We also ask forgiveness for our sins and beg the Father's blessing upon us and all human beings.

OUTLINE OF THE MASS

The Introductory Rites

THE Eucharist consists of the Liturgy of the Word and the Liturgy of the Eucharist plus introductory and concluding rites.

During the Introductory Rites acts of prayer and penitence prepare us to meet Christ as He comes in Word and Sacrament. We gather as a worshiping community to celebrate our unity with and in Him.

The Liturgy of the Word

THE proclamation of God's Word is always centered on Christ. Jesus is the Word of God Himself and the Author of Revelation. It is He Himself Who speaks to us when the Sacred Scriptures are liturgically proclaimed, and He calls for our positive response.

The Liturgy of the Eucharist

WE enter now into the Eucharistic sacrifice itself, the Supper of the Lord. We are God's new people, the redeemed brothers and sisters of Christ, gathered around His table.

Preparation of the Gifts

WE bring forward our gifts of bread and wine as well as our monetary offerings for the upkeep of the church building and the clergy, and the relief of the poor. These are but a symbol of our inner readiness to give God all of ourselves with our hopes and disappointments, our work and leisure, and our whole everyday lives.

Eucharistic Prayer

THE Eucharistic service of praise and thanksgiving is the center of the celebration. We join Christ in His sacrifice, celebrating His memorial and acknowledging the wonderful works of God in our lives.

At the consecration of the bread and wine Christ's words spoken through the priest accomplish what they signify: His Eucharistic Body and Blood, His Real Presence with all the riches of the Kingdom.

The people now praise Christ in the Memorial Acclamation. We celebrate the fact that Christ has redeemed us, is with us now to apply that Redemption to each of us, and will return in glory to perfect that Redemption for all.

The Communion Rite

THE Communion Rite is the conclusion of the Mass. It is the part when God gives a gift to us after we have presented our gift to Him: Jesus Christ, the Son of God and Savior of the world. We receive the Body and Blood, Soul and Divinity of Jesus

Christ, the Bread of Life, that gives access to eternity.

The Concluding Rites

WE have heard God's Word and responded to it. We have received Christ's Body and Blood and achieved greater union with Him and others. Now we leave to praise and bless the Lord in our daily lives.

Prayer before Mass

ETERNAL Father, I offer You the sacrifice wherein Your dear Son Jesus offered Himself upon the Cross, and which He now renews upon this altar, to adore You and to render to You that honor which is Your due, acknowledging our supreme dependence on You. You are our first beginning and our last end.

I offer it to give You thanks for the many benefits I have received, to appease Your justice provoked by so many sins of people, and to offer You worthy satisfaction for them, and finally to implore Your grace and mercy for myself, for all those who are in trouble and distress, for all poor sinners, for the whole world and for the souls in purgatory.

Prayer after Mass

O God, Your mercies are without number and Your goodness is an infinite treasure. I render thanks to Your most gracious Majesty for the gifts You have bestowed upon us.

At the same time, I also implore Your mercy, that as You grant the prayers of those that ask You, You will never forsake them, but will prepare them for the future reward. Through Christ our Lord. Amen.

DAILY PRAYERS

The Sign of the Cross

IN the name of the Father, and of the Son, ✠ and of the Holy Spirit. Amen.

The Lord's Prayer

OUR Father, Who art in heaven, hallowed be Thy name; Thy kingdom come, Thy will be done on earth as it is in heaven. Give us this day our daily bread, and forgive us our trespasses, as we forgive those who trespass against us; and lead us not into temptation, but deliver us from evil. Amen.

The Hail Mary

HAIL, Mary, full of grace! The Lord is with thee; blessed art thou among women, and blessed is the fruit of thy womb, Jesus.

Holy Mary, Mother of God, pray for us sinners now and at the hour of our death. Amen.

Glory Be to the Father

GLORY be to the Father, and to the Son, and to the Holy Spirit. As it was in the beginning, is now, and ever shall be. Amen.

The Apostles' Creed

I believe in God, the Father Almighty, Creator of heaven and earth, and in Jesus Christ, His only Son, Our Lord, Who was conceived by the Holy Spirit, born of the Virgin Mary, suffered under Pontius Pilate, was crucified, died and was buried; He descended into hell; on the third day He rose again from the dead; He ascended into heaven, and is seated at the right hand of God the Father Almighty; from there

He will come to judge the living and the dead.

I believe in the Holy Spirit, the holy catholic Church, the communion of saints, the forgiveness of sins, the resurrection of the body, and life everlasting. Amen.

An Act of Faith

O my God, I firmly believe that You are one God in three Divine Persons, Father, Son, and Holy Spirit. I believe that Your Divine Son became Man, and died for our sins, and He will come to judge the living and the dead.

I believe these and all the truths that the Holy Catholic Church teaches because You have revealed them, Who can neither deceive nor be deceived.

An Act of Hope

O my God, relying on Your almighty power and infinite

mercy and promises, I hope to obtain pardon for my sins, the help of Your grace, and life everlasting, through the merits of Jesus Christ, my Lord and Redeemer.

An Act of Love

O my God, I love You above all things, with my whole heart and soul, because You are all-good and worthy of all love.

I love my neighbor as myself for the love of You. I forgive all who have injured me, and ask pardon of all whom I have injured.

An Act of Contrition

O my God, I am heartily sorry for having offended You, and I detest all my sins because of Your just punishments, but most of all because they offend You, my God, Who are all-good and deserving of all my love. I firmly resolve, with the help of Your grace, to sin no more and to avoid the unnecessary occasions of sin. Amen.

Prayer to the Holy Spirit

COME, Holy Spirit, fill the hearts of Your faithful and kindle in them the fire of Your love.

℣. Send forth Your Spirit, and they shall be created.

℟. And You shall renew the face of the earth.

Let us pray. O God, You instructed the hearts of the faithful by the light of the Holy Spirit. Grant that, by the gift of the same Spirit, we may be always truly wise, and ever rejoice in His consolation. Through Christ our Lord. Amen.

The Angelus

℣. The Angel of the Lord declared unto Mary.

℟. And she conceived of the Holy Spirit.

Hail Mary, etc.

℣. Behold the handmaid of the Lord.

℟. Be it done unto me according to your word.

Hail Mary, etc.

℣. And the Word was made flesh.

℟. And dwelt among us.

Hail Mary, etc.

℣. Pray for us, O holy Mother of God.

℟. That we may be made worthy of the promises of Christ.

Let us pray. Pour forth, we beseech You, O Lord, Your grace into our hearts, that we to whom the Incarnation of Christ, Your

Son, was made known by the message of an Angel, may by His Passion and Cross be brought to the glory of His Resurrection, through the same Christ our Lord. Amen.

Regina Caeli

(Said during Eastertide instead of Angelus)

QUEEN of heaven, rejoice, alleluia. For He Whom you merited to bear, alleluia.
Has risen as He said, alleluia.
Pray for us to God, alleluia.

℣. Rejoice and be glad, O Virgin Mary, alleluia.

℟. Because the Lord is truly risen, alleluia.

Let us pray. O God, by the Resurrection of Your Son, our Lord Jesus Christ, You granted joy to the whole world. Grant, we beg You, that, through the intercession of the Virgin Mary, His Mother, we may attain the joys of eternal life. Through the same Christ our Lord. Amen.

Hail, Holy Queen

HAIL, Holy Queen, Mother of mercy, hail, our life, our sweetness, and our hope! To you do we cry, poor banished children of Eve! To you do we send up our sighs, mourning, and weeping in this vale of tears!

Turn then, most gracious advocate, your eyes of mercy toward us; and after this, our exile, show unto us the blessed fruit of your womb, Jesus! O clement, O loving, O sweet Virgin Mary!

Blessing before Meals

BLESS us, O Lord, and these Your gifts, which we are about to receive from Your bounty, through Christ our Lord. Amen.

Grace after Meals

WE give You thanks for all Your benefits, O Almighty God, Who live and reign forever. Amen.

May the souls of the faithful departed, through the mercy of God, rest in peace. Amen.

Act of Spiritual Communion

MY Jesus, I believe that You are in the Blessed Sacrament. I love You above all things, and I long for You in my soul. Since I cannot now receive You sacramentally, come at least spiritually into my heart.

I know You have already come. I embrace You and unite myself entirely to You; never permit me to be separated from You.

MORNING PRAYERS

Offering to the Trinity

MOST holy and adorable Trinity, one God in three Persons, I praise You and give You thanks for all the favors You have bestowed upon me. Your goodness has preserved me until now. I offer You my whole being and in particular all my thoughts, words and deeds, together with all the trials I may undergo this day.

Give them Your blessing. May Your Love animate them and may they serve Your greater glory.

I make this morning offering in union with the Divine intentions of Jesus Christ Who offers Himself daily in the holy Sacrifice of the Mass, and in union with Mary, His Virgin Mother and our Mother, who was always the faithful handmaid of the Lord.

Glory be to the Father, and to the Son, and to the Holy Spirit. Amen.

Prayer for Divine Guidance through the Day

LORD, God Almighty, You have brought us safely to the beginning of this day. Defend us today by Your mighty power, that we may not fall into any sin, but that all our words may so proceed and all our thoughts and actions be so directed, as to be always just in Your sight.

Direct, we beg you, O Lord, our actions by Your holy inspirations, and carry them on by Your gracious assistance, that every prayer and work of ours may begin always with You, and through You be happily ended. Amen.

NIGHT PRAYERS

Prayer to the Trinity

I adore You, my God, and thank You for having created me, for having made me a Christian and preserved me this day. I love You with all my heart and I am sorry for having sinned against You, because You are infinite Love and infinite Goodness. Protect me during my rest and may Your love be always with me.

Eternal Father, I offer You the Precious Blood of Jesus in atonement for my sins and for all the intentions of our Holy Church.

Holy Spirit, Love of the Father and the Son, purify my heart and fill it with the fire of Your Love, so that I may be a chaste Temple of the Holy Trinity and be always pleasing to You in all things. Amen.

Plea for Divine Help

HEAR us, Lord, holy Father, almighty and eternal God; and graciously send Your holy Angel from heaven to watch over, to cherish, to protect, to abide with, and to defend all who dwell in this house. Through Christ our Lord. Amen.

Prayer to One's Guardian Angel

ANGEL of God, my guardian dear, to whom His love entrusts me here, ever this night be at my side, to light and guard, to rule and guide. Amen.

Jesus, Mary, Joseph

JESUS, Mary, Joseph, I give You my heart and my soul. Jesus, Mary, Joseph, assist me in my last agony. Jesus, Mary, Joseph, may I sleep and rest in peace with You. Amen.

CONFESSION PRAYERS

WHEN we go to confession, we should:

(1) *Ask ourselves how we have offended God.* (2) *Be truly sorry for our sins.* (3) *Make up our minds not to sin again.* (4) *Tell our sins to the priest.* (5) *Do the penance the priest gives us.*

Prayer before Confession

MY Lord and God, I have sinned. I am guilty before You. Grant me the strength to say to Your minister what I say to You in the secret of my heart.

Increase my repentance. Make it more genuine. May it be really a sorrow for having offended You and my neighbor rather than a wounded love of self.

Help me to atone for my sin. May the sufferings of my life and my little mortifications be joined with the sufferings of Jesus, Your Son, and cooperate in rooting sin from the world.

Thanksgiving after Confession

MY dearest Jesus, I have told all my sins as well as I could. I have tried hard to make a good confession. I feel sure that You have forgiven me. I thank You. It is only because of all Your sufferings that I can go to confession and free myself from my sins. Your Heart is full of love and mercy for poor sinners. I love You because You are so good to me.

My loving Savior, I shall try to keep from sin and to love You more each day. My dear Mother Mary, pray for me and help me to keep my promises. Protect me and do not let me fall back into sin.

PRAYERS BEFORE COMMUNION

Act of Faith

LORD Jesus Christ, I firmly believe that You are present in this Blessed Sacrament as true God and true Man, with Your Body and Blood, Soul and Divinity. My Redeemer and my Judge, I adore Your Divine Majesty together with the Angels and Saints. I believe, O Lord; increase my faith.

Act of Hope

GOOD Jesus, in You alone I place all my hope. You are my salvation and my strength, the Source of all good. Through Your mercy, through Your Passion and Death, I hope to obtain the pardon of my sins, the grace of final perseverance, and a happy eternity.

Act of Love

JESUS, my God, I love You with my whole heart and above all things, because You are the one supreme Good and an infinitely perfect Being.

You have given Your life for me, a poor sinner, and in Your mercy You have even offered Yourself as food for my soul. My God, I love You. Inflame my heart so that I may love You more.

Act of Contrition

O my Savior, I am truly sorry for having offended You because You are infinitely good and sin displeases You. I detest all the sins of my life and I desire to atone for them.

Through the merits of Your Precious Blood, wash from my soul all stain of sin, so that, cleansed in body and soul, I may worthily approach the Most Holy Sacrament of the Altar.

Act of Desire

JESUS, my God and my all, my soul longs for You. My heart yearns to receive You in Holy Communion. Come, Bread of Heaven and Food of Angels, to nourish my soul and to rejoice my heart. Come, most lovable Friend of my soul, to inflame me with such love that I may never again be separated from You.

PRAYERS AFTER COMMUNION

Act of Faith

JESUS, I firmly believe that You are present within me as God and Man, to enrich my soul with graces and to fill my heart with the happiness of the blessed. I believe that You are Christ, the Son of the living God!

Act of Adoration

WITH deepest humility, I adore You, my Lord and God; You have made my soul Your dwelling place. I adore You as my Creator from Whose hands I came and with Whom I long to be happy forever.

Act of Love

DEAR Jesus, I love You with my whole heart, my whole soul, and all my strength. May the love of Your own Sacred Heart fill my soul and purify it so that I may die to the world for love of You, as You died on the Cross for love of me. My God, You are all mine; grant that I may be all Yours in time and in eternity.

Act of Thanksgiving

FROM the depths of my heart I thank You, dear Lord, for Your infinite kindness in coming to me. How good You are to me! With Your most holy Mother and all the Angels, I praise Your mercy and generosity toward me, a poor sinner. I thank You for nourishing my soul with Your Sacred Body and Precious Blood.

I will try to show my gratitude to You in the Sacrament of Your love, by obedience to Your holy commandments, by fidelity to my duties, by kindness to my neighbor, and by an earnest endeavor to become like You in my daily conduct.

Prayer to Christ the King

O CHRIST Jesus, I acknowledge You as King of the universe. All that has been created has been made for You. Exercise upon me all Your rights.

I renew my baptismal promises, renouncing Satan and all his works and pomps. I promise to live a good Christian life and to be diligent in furthering the interests and teachings of Almighty God and Your Church.

Prayer to Our Redeemer

SOUL of Christ, sanctify me. Body of Christ, save me. Water from the side of Christ, wash me. Blood of Christ, motivate me. Passion of Christ, strengthen me. O good Jesus, hear me.

Within Your wounds hide me. Suffer me not to be separated from You. From the malignant enemy, defend me. At the hour of death, call me. And bid me come to You, that with Your Saints I may praise You, forever and ever.

Prayer to Jesus Christ Crucified

BEHOLD O kind and most sweet Jesus, I cast myself upon my knees in Your sight, and with the most fervent desire of my soul I pray and beseech You that You would impress upon my heart lively sentiments of Faith, Hope, and Charity, with true repentance for my sins, and a firm desire of amendment, while with deep affection and grief of soul I ponder within myself and mentally contemplate Your five most precious wounds; having before my eyes that which David spoke in prophecy of You, O good Jesus: They have pierced My Hands and feet; they have numbered all My bones.

PRAYERS FOR EVERY DAY OF THE WEEK

Sunday

The Most Holy Trinity

MOST blessed Trinity, Father, Son, and Holy Spirit, behold us kneeling in Your Divine presence. We humble ourselves deeply and beg of You the forgiveness of our sins. We adore You, almighty Father, and with all our hearts we thank You for having given us Your Divine Son Jesus to be our Redeemer.

We adore You, Word of God, Jesus our Redeemer, and with all our hearts we thank You for having taken human flesh upon Yourself and having become priest and victim for our redemption in the sacrifice of the Cross, a sacrifice that, through Your great love, You renew upon our altars.

We adore you, Divine Spirit, and with all our hearts we thank You for having worked the unfathomable mystery of the Incarnation of the Word of God with such great love for us, a blessing that is being continually extended and increased in the Sacrament of the Eucharist. By this adorable mystery grant us and all poor sinners Your holy grace. Pour forth Your sacred gifts upon us and upon all redeemed souls.

Monday

The Holy Spirit

O Holy Spirit, Divine Paraclete, Father of the poor, Consoler of the afflicted, and Sanctifier of souls, behold us prostrate in Your presence. We adore You with deepest submission and we repeat with the seraphim who stand before Your throne; "Holy, holy, holy!"

You filled the soul of Mary with immense graces and inflamed the hearts of the apostles with holy zeal; enkindle our hearts with Your love. You are a supernatural light; enlighten us that we may understand eternal things. You appeared as a dove; grant us purity of life.

You came as a wind full of sweetness; disperse the storms of passion that rise in us. You appeared as a tongue; teach us to sing Your praises without ceasing. You came forth in a cloud; cover us with the shade of Your protection.

O Bestower of heavenly gifts, vivify us by Your grace, sanctify us by Your love, and govern us by Your infinite mercy, so that we may never cease blessing, praising, and loving You now during our earthly lives and later in heaven for all eternity.

Tuesday

All Angels and Saints

HEAVENLY Father, in praising Your Angels and Saints we praise Your glory, for by honoring them we honor You, their Creator. Their splendor shows us Your greatness, which infinitely surpasses that of all creation.

In Your loving providence, You saw fit to send Your Angels to watch over us. Grant that we may always be under their protection and one day enjoy their company in heaven.

Heavenly Father, You are glorified in Your Saints, for their glory is the crowning of Your gifts. You provide an example for us by their lives on earth,

You give us their friendship by our communion with them, You grant us strength and protection through their prayer for the Church, and You spur us on to victory over evil and the prize of eternal glory by this great company of witnesses.

Grant that we who aspire to take part in their joy may be filled with the Spirit that blessed their lives, so that, after sharing their faith on earth, we may also experience their peace in heaven.

Wednesday

St. Joseph

HOLY Joseph, you were always most just; make us relish what is right. You sustained Jesus and Mary in time of trial; sustain us by your help. You provided for all the needs of Jesus and Mary; help the needy of the whole world. You rescued Jesus from Herod who sought to kill Him; save us from our many sins.

You were the foster father of Christ, the priest-victim; make priests faithful to their calling. You were the foster father of Christ, the Divine physician; sustain the sick and obtain relief for them. You died the holiest of deaths in the arms of Jesus and Mary; intercede for the dying. You were the intrepid guardian of the Holy Family; protect all Christian families.

You cared for Jesus with true fatherly love; protect all children in the world. You were a dedicated and honest worker in your trade as a carpenter; teach us to labor for Jesus. You were the faithful and chaste spouse of the Blessed Virgin Mary; preserve in all hearts a love of fidelity and purity. You were a model single person and a model father later on; help all human beings to imitate your virtues.

Thursday

The Blessed Sacrament

LORD Jesus, at the Last Supper as You sat at table with Your Apostles, You offered Yourself to the Father as the spotless lamb, the acceptable gift that renders perfect praise to Him. You have given us the memorial of Your Passion to bring us its saving power until the end of time. In this great Sacrament You feed Your people and strengthen them in holiness, so that the human family may come to walk in the light of one faith, and in one communion of love. We are fed at Your table and grow into Your risen likeness.

Lord Jesus, You are the Eternal and True Priest Who established this unending sacrifice. You offered Yourself as a Victim for our deliverance and You taught us to offer it throughout time in memory of You. As we eat Your Body that You gave for us, we grow in strength. As we drink Your Blood that You poured out for us, we are washed clean.

Lord Jesus, let the power of Your Eucharist pervade every aspect of our daily lives. Let Your consecration transform all our actions and all the events of each day into supernatural agents that form Your Mystical Body.

Friday

The Holy Cross

LORD Jesus, from the height of Your throne of suffering

You reveal the depth of Your love for us. Lifted up from the world on the Cross, You draw everyone to Yourself.

The Cross is both the symbol and the act by which You raised up the world from all its sin and weakness. But You also ask for our cooperation.

Help us to die to self so that we may live for You and our fellow human beings. Set us free from the slavery of our passions, our prejudices, and our selfishness. Enable us to endure the pains and trials of this life and really help to change the world in our own small way.

Keep before our minds the conviction that in the Cross is salvation and life as well as defense against our enemies. Through the Cross heavenly grace is given us, our minds are strengthened, and we experience spiritual joy. In the Cross is the height of virtue and the perfection of all sanctity. Let us take up our Cross, and follow You through earthly sorrow into eternal happiness in heaven.

Saturday

The Blessed Virgin Mary

VIRGIN Mother of God, most august Mother of the Church, we commend the whole Church to you.

You bear the sweet name of "Help of Bishops"; keep the bishops in your care, and be at their side and at the side of the priests, religious, and laity who offer them help in sustaining the difficult work of the pastoral office.

From the Cross, the Divine Savior, your Son, gave you as a most loving Mother to the disciple whom He loved; remember the Christian people who commit themselves to you.

Be mindful of all your children; join to their prayers your special power and authority with God. Keep their faith whole and lasting, strengthen their hope, and enkindle their love. Come to the aid of those who find themselves in hardship, in need, in danger, and especially those who are suffering persecution.

We commend the whole human race to your Immaculate Heart, O Virgin Mother of God. Lead it to acknowledge Jesus as the one true Savior. Drive far from it all the calamities provoked by sin. Bring it peace, which consists in truth, justice, liberty, and love.

PRAYERS FOR LITURGICAL TIMES

Advent

Prayer for Christ's Triple Coming

LAMB of God, You once came to rid the world of sin; cleanse me now of every stain of sin. Lord, You came to save what was lost; come once again with Your salvific power so that those You redeemed will not be punished. I have come to know You in faith; may I have unending joy when You come again in glory.

Christmas Time

Prayer to Jesus, God's Greatest Gift

O Jesus, I believe that the greatest proof of God's love is His gift to us of You, His only Son. All love tends to become like that which it loves. You love human beings; therefore You became man. Infinite love and mercy caused You, the Second Person of the Blessed Trinity, to leave the Kingdom of eternal bliss, to descend from the throne of Your majesty, and to become a helpless babe. Eventually You even suffered and died and rose that we might live.

You wished to enter the world as a child in order to show that You were true Man. But You become man also that we may become like God. In exchange for the humanity that You take from us You wish to make us share in Your Divinity by sanctifying grace, so that You may take sole possession of us. Grant me the grace to love You in return with a deep, personal, and productive love.

Lent

Prayer to Be Freed of the Seven Deadly Sins

O meek Savior and Prince of Peace, implant in me the virtues of gentleness and patience. Let me curb the fury of anger and restrain all resentment and impatience so as to overcome evil with good, attain Your peace, and rejoice in Your love.

O Model of humility, divest me of all pride and arrogance. Let me acknowledge my weakness and sinfulness, so that I may bear mockery and contempt for Your sake and esteem myself as lowly in Your sight.

O Teacher of abstinence, help me to serve You rather than my appetites. Keep me from gluttony—the inordinate love of food and drink—and let me hunger and thirst for Your justice.

O Lover of purity, remove all lust from my heart, so that I may serve You with a pure mind and a chaste body.

O Father of the poor, help me to avoid all covetousness for earthly goods and give me a love for heavenly things. Inspire me to give to the needy, just as You gave Your life that I might inherit eternal treasures.

O Exemplar of love, keep me from all envy and ill-will. Let the grace of Your love dwell in me that I may rejoice in the happiness of others and bewail their adversities.

O zealous Lover of souls, keep me from all sloth of mind or body. Inspire me with zeal for Your glory, so that I may do all things for You and in You.

Prayer of Contrition

MERCIFUL Father, I am guilty of sin. I confess my sins before You and I am sorry for them. Your promises are just; therefore I trust that You will forgive me my sins and cleanse me from every stain of sin. Jesus Himself is the propitiation for my sins and those of the whole world. I put my hope in His atonement. May my sins be forgiven through His Name, and in His Blood may my soul be made clean.

Easter Time

Prayer in Praise of Christ's Humanity

O risen Lord, Your Body was part of Your power, rather than You a part in its weakness. For this reason You could not but rise again, if You were to die—

because Your Body, once taken by You, never was or could be separated from You even in the grave.

I keep Your most holy Body before me as the pledge of my own resurrection. Though I die, it only means that my life is changed, for I shall rise again.

Teach me to live as one who believes in the great dignity and sanctity of the material frame that You have given to me.

Ordinary Time

Prayer for a Productive Faith

O Lord, increase my faith and let it bear fruit in my life. Let it bind me fast to other Christians in the common certitude that our Master is the God-Man Who gave His life for all. Let me listen in faith to the Divine word that challenges me.

Help me to strive wholeheartedly under the promptings of my faith in the building of a world ruled by love. Enable me to walk in faith toward the indescribable future that You have promised to all who possess a productive faith in You.

Prayer to Christ in the World

LORD Jesus, let us realize that every action of ours no matter how small or how secular enables us to be in touch with You. Let our interest lie in created things—but only in absolute dependence upon Your presence in them. Let us pursue You and You alone through the reality of created things. Let this be our prayer—to become closer to You by becoming more human.

Let us become a true branch on the vine that is You, a branch that bears much fruit. Let us accept You in our lives in the way it pleases You to come into them: as Truth, to be spoken; as Life, to be lived; as Light, to be shared; as Love, to be followed; as Joy, to be given; as Peace, to be spread about; as Sacrifice, to be offered among our relatives and friends, among our neighbors and all people.

PRAYERS TO OUR BLESSED MOTHER

(See also pp. 17-19)

We Fly to Your Patronage

WE fly to your patronage, O holy Mother of God; despise not our petitions in our necessities, but deliver us always from all dangers, O glorious and blessed Virgin.

The "Memorare"

REMEMBER, O most gracious Virgin Mary, that never was it known that anyone who fled to your protection, implored your help or sought your intercession was left unaided.

Inspired with this confidence, I fly to you, O Virgin of virgins, my Mother; to you do I come, before you I stand, sinful and sorrowful. O Mother of the Word Incarnate, despise not my petitions, but in your mercy hear and answer me. Amen.

How to Say the Rosary

1. Begin on the crucifix and say the Apostles' Creed.
2. On the 1st bead, say 1 Our Father.
3. On the next 3 beads, say Hail Mary.

4. Next say 1 Glory Be. Then announce and think of the first Mystery and what it means, and say 1 Our Father.
5. Say 10 Hail Marys and 1 Glory be to the Father.
6. Announce the second Mystery and continue in the same way until each of the five Mysteries of the selected group or decade is said.

The Joyful Mysteries

1. The Angel Gabriel brings the joyful message to Mary.
2. Mary visits her cousin Elizabeth.
3. Jesus is born in a stable in Bethlehem.
4. Jesus is offered in the Temple.
5. Jesus is found again in the Temple.

The Luminous Mysteries

1. Jesus is baptized in the Jordan.
2. Jesus reveals Himself at Cana.
3. Jesus proclaims God's Kingdom.
4. Jesus is transfigured.
5. Jesus institutes the Eucharist.

The Sorrowful Mysteries

1. Jesus prays in agony to His Heavenly Father.
2. Jesus is scourged.
3. Jesus is crowned with thorns.
4. Jesus carries His Cross to Calvary.
5. Jesus dies on the Cross.

The Glorious Mysteries

1. Jesus rises from death.
2. Jesus ascends to Heaven.
3. The Holy Spirit descends upon the Apostles.
4. Mary is taken up to Heaven in body and soul.
5. Mary is crowned in Heaven.

PRAYERS TO THE SAINTS

Prayer to St. Michael the Archangel

ST. Michael the Archangel, defend us in the day of battle; be our safeguard against the wiles and wickedness of the devil. May God rebuke him, we humbly pray, and do thou, O prince of the heavenly host, by the power of God cast into hell Satan and all the other evil spirits, who prowl through the world, seeking the ruin of souls.

Prayer to One's Guardian Angel

Daily Protector throughout Life

DEAR Angel, in His goodness God gave you to me to guide, protect, and enlighten me, and to bring me back to the right way when I go astray.

Encourage me when I am disheartened, and instruct me when I err in my judgment. Help me to become more Christlike, and so some day to be accepted into the company of Angels and Saints in heaven.

Prayer to St. Anne

Patroness of Homemakers

DEAR Saint, we know nothing about you except your name. But you gave us the Mother of God who called herself handmaid of the Lord. In your home you raised the Queen of Heaven and are rightly the model of homemakers.

In your womb came to dwell the new Eve uniquely conceived without sin. Intercede for us that we too may remain free from sin.

Prayer to St. Monica

Patroness of Mothers

EXEMPLARY Mother of the great Augustine, you perseveringly pursued your wayward son with love and affection and pardon and counsel and powerful cries to heaven.

Intercede for all mothers in our day so that they may learn to draw their children to God. Teach them how to remain close to their children, even the prodigal sons and daughters who have sadly gone astray.

Prayer to St. Thérèse of the Child Jesus

Patroness of Missionaries

DEAR Little Flower of Lisieux, how wonderful was the short life you led. Though cloistered, you went far and wide through fervent prayers and great sufferings. You obtained from God untold helps and graces for his evangelists.

Help all missionaries and teach all of us to spread Christianity in our own neighborhoods and family circles.

Prayer to St. Christopher

Patron of Motorists

DEAR Saint, you have inherited a beautiful name ("Christbearer") as a result of a wonderful legend that while carrying people across a raging stream you also carried the Child Jesus.

Teach us to be true Christbearers to those who do not know Him. Protect drivers, who transport those who bear Christ within them.

Prayer to St. Francis of Assisi

Patron of the World

DEAR Saint, once worldly and vain, you became humble and poor for the sake of Jesus and had an extraordinary love for the Crucified, which showed itself in your body by the imprints of Christ's Wounds.

In our selfish age, how greatly we need your secret that draws countless men and women to imitate you. Teach us also great love for the poor and unswerving loyalty to the Vicar of Christ.

Prayer to St. Jude

Patron of Desperate Causes

ST. Jude, apostle of Christ, the Church honors and prays to you universally as the patron of hopeless and difficult cases. Pray for us in our needs. Make use, we implore you, of this powerful privilege given to you to bring visible and speedy help where help is needed. Pray that we humbly accept the trials and disappointments and mistakes that are a part of our human nature.

Let us see the reflection of the sufferings of Christ in our daily trials and tribulations. Let us see in a spirit of great faith and hope the part we even now share in the joy of Christ's Resurrection, and which we long to share fully in heaven. Intercede that we may again experience this joy in answer to our present needs if it is God's desire for us. *(Here make your request.)*

We know our prayers will be heard through your intercession.

Prayer to St. Anthony

Patron of the Poor

O holy St. Anthony, gentlest of Saints, your love for God and charity for His creatures made you worthy even on earth to possess miraculous powers. Miracles waited on your word, which you were ever ready to speak for those in trouble or anxiety. Encouraged by this thought, I implore you to obtain for me my request *(here mention your intention).*

The answer to my prayer may require a miracle; even so, you are the Saint of miracles. O gentle and loving St. Anthony, whose heart is ever full of human sympathy, whisper my petition into the ears of the sweet Infant Jesus, Who loved to be enfolded in your arms, and the gratitude of my heart will be ever yours.

Prayer to St. Rita

Patroness of Impossible Cases

HOLY Patroness of those in need, St. Rita, your pleadings before your Divine Lord are irresistible. For your lavishness in granting favors you have been called the "Advocate of the Hopeless" and even of the "Impossible." You are so humble, so mortified, so patient, and so compassionate in love for your crucified Jesus that you can obtain from Him anything you ask if it is His Holy Will. Therefore, all confidently have recourse to you in the hope of comfort or relief.

Be propitious toward your suppliants and show your power with God in their behalf. Be generous with your favors now as you have been in so many wonderful cases for the greater glory of God, the spread of your devotion, and the consolation of those who trust in you. We promise, if our petition be granted, to glorify you by making known your favor, and to bless you and sing your praises. Relying then on your merits and power before the Sacred Heart of Jesus, we ask of you *(here mention your request).*

Prayer to St. Patrick

Patron of Ireland

DEAR St. Patrick, in your humility you called yourself a sinner, but you became a most successful missionary and prompted countless pagans to follow the Savior. Many of their descendants in turn spread the Good News in numerous foreign lands. Through your powerful intercession with God, obtain for us the missionaries we need to continue the work you began.